PRAYER HANDBOOK

FOR

CHAPLAINS

MINISTERS

FIRST RESPONDERS

HEALTH CARE PROVIDERS

America Selby

Ladies Image Publishing

Email: americaselby.com

Dear Reader,

If you enjoyed this book or found it useful, I would be very grateful if you would post a short review on Amazon. Your support really does make a difference and I read all the reviews personally so I can get your feedback and make this book even better.

If you are a member of kindleunlimited, I would be most grateful if you would scroll to the back of the book so I will be paid for your borrowed book.

Thanks again for your support.

America Selby

PRAYER WITH A FAMILY AFTER A DEATH OF A LOVED ONE

Death is one of the great mysteries of life, and also one of the greatest sources of grief for those who are left behind. Because the death of a loved one is such a tender time, it is especially important to be sensitive to the family's own beliefs and desires during this circumstance. You would not want to pray about the afterlife if the family does not believe in the afterlife. Neither would you want to claim any assurance that is actually not comforting to the family. There are some other big faux pas in certain religions. For instance, some Muslims believe if the deceased is an unbeliever, that praying for them is forbidden and punishable. For all of these reasons, it is important to be sensitive. At the same time, you want to acknowledge the hope onto which the family is clinging so that each person can be reminded of their source of strength. You can ascertain these facts by asking questions such as: "Is there anything that gives you comfort during this difficult and sad circumstance?" "Do you come from a certain faith or denomination that helps you during these tender times?" "I only got to know *the deceased's name* a little, can you tell me more about them?" These questions can provide comfort, provide a chance for people to reminisce, as well as help you add details to the prayers to make them more personal.

You will also note in the following prayers that euphemisms such as "pass away" or "loss" are not used. It is common practice by hospital and hospice chaplains to use the word death when somebody dies. It acknowledges the reality and pain of the situation and is important for the family as they start the healing process. You will also note that the prayer talks about both the family and the person who has died.

When families are dealing with the death of a loved one, they generally need a way to honor the life of the one who has died, note their hopes for the person who has died, and claim their needs for comfort, forgiveness, or whatever other feelings they might be harboring.

A Christian Prayer

Prince of Peace and Mighty Comforter, you promise us that you are present to us in life and in death. Nothing, not even death, can separate us from your love. So, we cling to this promise today, relying on you to be faithful still. The family of *deceased's name* loves *deceased's name* so very much. You love *deceased's name* even more, and loved them before they were even born. So, we pray that you are welcoming him/her with outstretched arms. God, we thank you for their life. We know that our world is not the same because *deceased's name* was in it, and we thank you for that. In the wake of their death, we ask that you would comfort their family with a peace that surpasses understanding. Be with them today, and in the days, months, and years ahead. Hear the cries of their heart and speak peace into their soul. Amen.

A Jewish Prayer

Elohim, you have been faithful to your people throughout all of human history. You were present to Abraham, Isaac, and Jacob. You were faithful to Sarah, Rahab and Naomi. You heard the cries of your people in Egypt, and now you hear our cries as we mourn. We come to lift prayers to you on behalf of *deceased's name*, thanking you for their life and praying for them after their death. While we mourn their death, we know that they have left their mark on our world. Indeed, the world is not the same because they were in it. So, now, eternal one, give shalom, your everlasting peace, to this family as they mourn. Be present to them as they grieve and as they remember. Today and every day that follows, we pray that you dry the tears from their eyes. We know that you mourn with us, and that our tears are matched with yours. So, as you join us, also provide us your comfort and care. Amen.

An Islamic Prayer

Allah, you are most powerful, the one God. Life and death rest in your hands. So in your power and mercy, be kindhearted to *deceased's name* and grant him/her forgiveness for any wrong they have done. Protect them and guide them after death, just as you offered guidance in life. We thank you for granting *deceased's name* the gift of life, and for the blessing that these people had of knowing them. For those who love *deceased's name,* be their companion as they face loneliness, be their comfort as they face grief, be their courage as they face difficult days ahead, and be their strength as they feel weak. We close in the words that the *deceased's name* has said so many times in their own prayer life*: p*eace be upon you and the mercy of Allah. Ameen.

A Buddhist Prayer

We dedicate this meditation to *deceased's name.* Earth-Store Bodhisattva, may you grant them peace and guide them after death. Most sacred Bodhisattvas and Buddhas, may *deceased's name* be granted compassion and be honored in the next life. As his/her family grieves, release them from the grief that holds them and give them comfort. May they have freedom and be granted loving kindness. We end in silent meditation, focusing on loving-kindness and asking that this be imbued to us today. May we experience peace. May we experience comfort. May we experience understanding. May we experience the love that *deceased name* offered throughout their life, even in their death.

PRAYER FOR HEALING

One of the most frequent things that patients request prayer for is healing. This is one way that people's spirituality can play into their care – spirituality can be just as much a part of a person's healing process as medicines and treatments. Therefore, praying with a patient can be an important part of the work that you do.

However, sometimes people have trouble praying these sort of prayers when a person's prognosis for healing is not good. Even when doctors have made it clear that healing is not an option for the patient, many people will continue to pray for healing for themselves or for their loved one. This is one of the ways that people hold onto hope, and while they might also have a realistic understanding of their prognosis, it does not mean that they have given up the hope or belief in miracles or healing. Joining people in prayers for healing is one of the basic ways that we can be present to people as they face illness and as they set about the meaningful task of valuing life, facing illness, or even dying.

A Christian Prayer

Healer God, when you walked this earth, you restored people with your touch and cured them with your words. People witnessed the miracles that you performed and were amazed. We believe that you still are a miracle worker, the Great Physician, the One by whom we can be healed. Lord, we pray that you use the work of the doctors and nurses to heal *patient's name*; I ask this for myself as I care for this patient. Give each caregiver knowledge and compassion as they treat *patient's name*. We also ask that you take away any pain and weakness that *patient's name* is experiencing. Give them strength as they heal, give them courage when they waver, give them rest when they tire, give them hope when they are distraught, give them perseverance when they lack gumption, and give them encouragement when they feel downtrodden. God, may today be a good day and a step in the right direction. All these prayers we lift to you in Jesus' name. Amen.

A Jewish Prayer

Adonai, in the beginning you breathed into the human form and created life. We ask that your breath now fill *patient's name*, and restore them to health. Give *patient's name* strength and healing. Give them hope and assurance. We ask that you restore them to full health, and that they feel better soon. Bless their doctors, nurses, and health care providers. Bless me with what I need to care for them well. Give us the knowledge to heal, the compassion to care well, and the tenderness to comfort. We also ask that you take away any pain and weakness that *patient's name* is experiencing. Give them strength as they heal, give them courage when they waver, give them rest when they tire, give them hope when they are distraught, give them perseverance when they lack gumption, and give them encouragement when they feel downtrodden. God, may today be a good day and a step in the right direction. Amen.

An Islamic Prayer:

Oh Sustainer God, we know that healing is yours and yours alone. You grant that your servants are healed and you are the one who restores them to health. Be gracious to *patient's name*, and heal them of their sickness. Protect them from pain and give them each good thing that they need during this time. Be present to them, as you are present to all of us during our lives. Soothe them; cure them; heal them; strengthen them. Allah, you are the one who grants favors and bestows us with blessing. We ask that you are abundant in these gifts. It is in worship and adoration that we make these requests. May your name be blessed. Ameen.

A Buddhist Prayer

As the sweet respite of summer rain mends cracked, arid ground, may *patient's name* mend and heal. May their pain be taken away. May they be restored to wholeness. May they be able to embrace the life that they knew before this illness, and return to activities they once did. When their energy wavers, may they be filled with glowing light that energizes and invigorates. When they grow distraught, may they be filled with hope. When they feel ill, may all sickness be taken from them. Though we never hope to grow ill or face times like these, may this be a reminder of the great gift of life and the beauty of health. May *patient's name* once again experience the joy of a healthy life. May it be so.

PRAYER FOR PATIENTS WHO ARE NEARING DEATH

As death approaches, people (if they are medically and mentally able to do so) tend to reflect on their life, seek meaning, and process their thoughts on death. It can be a time of anxiety or fear for a patient and/or their family as they confront the reality of what death might be. Surprisingly, it can also be a time of peace for people who come to terms with their own death. All of these prayers can be adapted to fit the feelings and attitudes of the patient and family. It is important to do so.

Additionally, you will note differences in the way these prayers cater to the varied understandings of the afterlife that exists in each religion. While these prayers are geared towards a general understanding of each religion's view of what follows death, it should be noted that these beliefs can vary widely from sect to sect, and person to person. As with all prayers, it would be beneficial to ascertain what the family believes and what is important to them.

A Christian Prayer

Alpha and Omega, beginning and end, you were with *patient's name* as they began their life, and remain with them now as they approach the end of their life. With the unknown of death looming large, *patient's name* is reflecting on their life and coming to terms with what they see. You know each detail of their life, so I pray that as they seek meaning, that you reveal what needs to be known. Give them understanding and assurance that you will not leave or forsake them in life or in death. Calm any anxiety that they may have, and give *patient's name* peace. Allow them to say the things they need to say to family and friends, and open up opportunities for others to speak to words of peace, forgiveness, understanding, and hope to *patient's name,* as well. May today and the days ahead be filled with holy moments, special time, and all that *patient's name* needs. We pray for your presence, oh Lord. Amen.

A Jewish Prayer

Great I-Am, the one who was, and is, and is to come – you were in the beginning and will be long after the end. You *are* with us now. So, we lift our eyes up to you YHWH, and pray for your presence in this specific moment of time. With the unknown of death looming large, *patient's name* is reflecting on their life and coming to terms with what they see. You know each detail of their life, so I pray that as they seek meaning, that you reveal what needs to be known. Give them understanding. Calm any anxiety, and give *patient's name* peace. Allow them to say the things they need to say to family, and friends, and open up opportunities for others to speak to words of peace, forgiveness, understanding, and hope to *patient's name,* as well. Reveal to them your presence and guide them in understanding. Amen.

An Islamic Prayer

There is no God but Allah, and Mohamed is his messenger. The world, including *patient's name's* life, rests in the dominion of the most high, and to Allah we turn in this time of struggle. As *patient's name* approaches death, they reflect on what they have done and not done, their moments of faithful obedience and wayward disobedience, their recognition of the Holy and times when they did not notice Allah in their presence. Allah, please remove any blemish that is not holy and cleanse *patient's name.* Help them prepare for death with comfort and assurance. Give them understanding. Calm any anxiety that they might have, and give *patient's name* peace. Allow them to say the things they need to say to family and friends, and open up opportunities for others to speak to words of peace, forgiveness, understanding, and hope to *patient's name,* as well. Reveal to them your presence and guide them in understanding. May it be so.

A Buddhist Prayer

As death draws nearer for all of us, but especially close for *patient's name*, we pause to reflect on the preciousness of life. Though our days are numbered, they are filled with chances like right now, to pause and reflect well – to leave a karmic imprint that will have a lasting effect – to claim the calm that is possible even in chaos. So, we pause to think positive thoughts and to reflect on the gift of life (*silence).* As *patient's name* seeks meaning, may he/she have understanding and peace. May he/she live into opportunities to think, act and speak good things to others. May these days be a blessing, and their soul be at peace. May good karma go with *patient's name* after death. Lift these thoughts, Buddha's and Bodhisattva's and grant your understanding.

PRAYER FOR RENEWED FAITH

Often as people are sick or facing death, they see their religious beliefs and practices in a new light. Some may interpret sickness as judgment, and they may want to renew their faith to counteract this judgment. This can be especially prevalent in conservative Christian beliefs. Others may view sickness as the opportunity to reflect anew; sickness might be interpreted as the wake-up call to live more faithfully into their religious practice. Often prayers for renewed faith can be relevant for those who are sick, hospitalized or facing death. This sort of prayer can also be relevant for care providers whose faith is challenged by what they see. Renewal of faith can come from all sorts of life circumstances. These prayers can be edited to incorporate whatever experience has led to this desire for a change in one's faith practices and/or beliefs.

A Christian Prayer

God who makes all things new, you have given us the gift of becoming new creations. Today, we embrace this gift and ask that you transform our hearts and minds. We have committed to following your ways, to live as Jesus would like us to live, and to be faithful disciples of your Word. We have fallen far short of that calling. So, forgive us of our waywardness and call us once again to come back into your fold. Renew *person's name's* faith. Restore their hope. Give them a new start. May the Holy Spirit breathe new life into their spiritual practices and beliefs. May they feel your presence and proclaim your truth. May you raise them as a disciples and bless them as they seek to serve you. Amen.

A Jewish Prayer

Creator God, you are the only one who can recreate us. So we come to you, asking for your grace and your forgiveness. *Person's name* wishes to renew their faith and recommit their life. The prophet Micah told us that it is good for us "to do justly, to love kindness, and to walk humbly with our God." While we may wish to live into this, we know that we have not done that perfectly. We have chosen ways that do not align with you, Adonai. So forgive us our waywardness and redirect our path. May we have the strength to be faithful and to stand boldly in faith. Just as Abraham and Sarah renewed their devotion to follow you when they turned astray, may our prayer also rise to you as a faithful offering and recommitment of our lives. Be with us as we seek to be faithful. Amen.

An Islamic Prayer

Al-Basir, all-seeing God, you have seen all of the deeds of our life – when we have followed Allah, and when we have gone astray. Forgive us for when you have seen unfaithfulness, and help us to be more faithful. Al-Sami', you are all-hearing. You have heard when we have spoken praise and when we have spoken curse. Forgive us for when we have not spoken words to glorify Allah, and renew our faith. Al-Hakim', all-wise God, you hold the wisdom of knowing what it will take for us to follow you. So, help us to follow you, and renew our faith. We declare what you have taught us – we affirm our belief in you. *Person's name* declares that they believe in Allah and believe in Mohamed as the prophet. They renew their faith. Hear this prayer. Amen.

A Buddhist Prayer

I dedicate this to the Buddha, to the Sangha, to the Dharma, and to myself. Each moment, each breath, offers the chance to live further into light and love. I take this moment to step more fully into true being and true light. May I reconnect with what is good, and through my practice sow what is good into the world. May I live simply and resist the temptations to focus on the materials of this world that hold me back from freedom. May I greet each gift with an open heart, but not grow attached to what might give me a false feeling of security. May I be a helper to my fellow humankind and to all of creation. May my meditation be pleasing and uplifting, starting a spark of light and love that might change myself and the world around me.

PRAYER ON HEARTBREAK FOR PATIENTS AND FAMILY

The colloquialism "heartbreak" so perfectly captures the heart-wrenching feeling that is caused in the most sorrow-evoking circumstances. When one truly experiences heartbreak, it feels as if the chest might rend open and pour out its contents. Heartbreak is most commonly associated with lost love, but the heart can break for a variety of circumstances, especially those tragic situations that people encounter when dealing with their own health failing, or the health of those they love being in question. These situations can also stir up people's emotional baggage, change existing relationships, and turn life on its head. Religions also speak to heartbreak, because religion has to do with both the head and the heart. The practice of one's religion is not just something done in the headspace, but a thing if the heart as well. In prayer, people are able to lift their own hearts up to meet God or the Holy. Hopefully, that is reflected in these prayers.

A Christian Prayer

Compassionate and loving Christ, when you were on this earth, you wept when your eyes filled with tears and your heart was full of sorrow. Your heart broke when those you loved were in pain, and when you were in pain. You know what it feels like to suffer heartbreak. So, join us today as we experience heartbreak. Especially be with *person's name*, providing them hope and a future. Speak comfort into the pain that they are feeling. Speak compassion to them as they are so vulnerable. Help give them peace around those circumstances that can have peace. Give them understanding around what can have understanding. Give them compassionate kindness around things that cannot be understood. God, I cannot understand what they are going through, but you do. So, be with them in every way that they need it. Amen.

A Jewish Prayer

The Psalms tell us that you are "near to the brokenhearted," so be near to *person's name* today. Speak comfort into the pain that they are feeling. Speak compassion to them as they are so vulnerable. Help give them peace around those circumstances that can have peace. Give them understanding around what can have understanding. Allow them to be compassionate around things that cannot be understood. God, I cannot understand what they are going through, but you do. So, be with them in every way that they need it. Be a presence in grief and a comfort in sorrow. Amen.

An Islamic Prayer

Allah, a heart that is hardened is a heart that is far from you. Yet, it is hard for a heart not to harden when faced with the sorrows of this world. So, in face of what is going on with *person's name*, we pray that you help them overcome it. Speak compassion to them as they are so vulnerable. Help give them peace around those circumstances that can have peace. Give them understanding around what can have understanding. Allow them to give themselves compassion around the things that cannot be understood. God, I cannot understand what they are going through, but you do. So, be with them in every way that they need it. Ameen.

A Buddhist Prayer

The world is full of suffering that can draw attention away from what is good and inspiring. Heartbreak is one of these things. It is so very real and can bring us more into the human spirit than the divine reality. So in face of all that is heartbreaking and dismaying, may *person's name* overcome what they face today. May they offer themselves compassion. May they have understanding about what can be understood. May they let go of whatever pain they can release. May they dance in lightness and find a future. May the Buddha help them be free.

PRAYER FOR HEARTBREAK FOR A HEALTHCARE WORKER

Often health care workers are told the most heart breaking stories, and their heart can wrench for the person that they have come to know through their job. While the patient might need prayers for their heartbreak, those that are caring for them also suffer the pain that they are experiencing indirectly. The healthcare worker can experience compassion fatigue as resonating with the patient and their family repeatedly hurts their heart. It, therefore, is essential for healthcare workers to be able to recognize their own heartbreak and be able to lift that up to the Holy. If these stresses and heartbreaks are not released, they get too heavy to bear. These prayers give voices to those feelings that healthcare workers experience second-handedly. They are similar to the prayers for patients written just above, but are not totally the same. These are prayers that you can offer for yourself or for fellow staff.

A Christian Prayer

Compassionate and loving Christ, when you were on this earth, you were not immune to the pain of this broken world, but welcomed all of what it means to be human. Your heart broke with those who were brokenhearted. So, join us today as we experience heartbreak on behalf of those people that we meet. Especially be with *staff's name* today. You have given them a compassionate heart that gives them the ability to be so kind to their patients and their families. Now, in their time of need, speak comfort into the pain that they are feeling. Speak compassion to them as they are so vulnerable. Help give them peace around those circumstances that can have peace. Give them understanding around what can have understanding. God, I cannot understand what they are going through, but you do. So, be with them in every way that they need it. Amen.

A Jewish Prayer

The Psalms tell us that you are "near to the brokenhearted," so be near to *staff's name* today. You have given them a heart that resembles yours – a heart that embraces people in relationships and feels their pain. This is a gift, but today does not particularly feel like it. So, speak comfort into the pain that they are feeling. Speak compassion to them as they are so vulnerable. Help give them peace around those circumstances that can have peace. Give them understanding around what can have understanding. Give them ways to let go of this pain that is holding them down. In just a moment of silence we remember the people for which this person mourns. Hear our prayers. Amen.

An Islamic Prayer

Allah, a heart that is hardened is a heart that is far from you. But, on days like today, it is tempting to harden our hearts so they do not feel this sort of pain. And yet, it is in this very moment that they are most resembling your heart. So, in face of the pain that *person's name* is experiencing, we pray that you help them overcome it. Speak compassion to them as they are so vulnerable. Help give them peace around those circumstances that can have peace. Give them understanding around what can have understanding. May the words that you have spoken through the prophets bless them with a peace of heart today. May they rest in you. Ameen.

A Buddhist Prayer

The world is full of suffering that can draw attention away from what is good and inspiring. Heartbreak is one of those things. And yet a compassionate heart opens us to the world. So, we are thankful for an open heart that greets the stranger and welcomes the friend. We hope that this heart is healed so that it might continue to greet the world. May *person's name* overcome what they face today. May they offer themselves compassion. May they have understanding about what can be understood. May they let go of whatever pain they can release. May they dance in lightness and find a future. May the Buddha help them be free.

PRAYER FOR YOUR NEW BABY'S FUTURE

One of the great joys of hospital work is seeing births. These great moments are also spaces where religion can voice what is in the heart. Prayers are not only a way to ask for healing, or peace in hard circumstances. They are also a way to recognize the blessings in life. When a baby is born, they have a whole future ahead of them. This holds great promise, but it also has a lot of unknowns. These prayers and meditations are a way to recognize both sides of that coin.

A Christian Prayer

God of new life, we thank you for the blessing of *baby's name*. There are perhaps no more earnest prayers than the silent look of awe that is expressed on the faces of family that cannot help but stare in wonder at this great gift of life. These prayers are lifted to you now, cast from the eyes of their parents and *other family members* and raised in reverence to you. Hear these prayers now. We also pray that you bless *baby's name* throughout his/her life, with great opportunity, with wellbeing, with love, and with hope. May they know more about you each day of their life. May they also experience the joy that this world has to offer. We thank you, God, for your faithfulness and the great gift of *baby's name*. Amen.

A Jewish Prayer

God of new life, we thank you for the blessing of *baby's name*. There are perhaps no more earnest prayers than the silent look of awe that is expressed on the faces of family that cannot help but stare in wonder at this great gift of life. These prayers are lifted to you now, cast from the eyes of their parents and *other family members* and raised in reverence to you. Hear these prayers now. We also pray that you bless *baby's name* throughout his/her life, with great opportunity, with wellbeing, with love, and with hope. You are the God who holds us in covenant relationship throughout his life. Hold *baby's* name in your care. Amen.

An Islamic Prayer

We greet *baby's name* with joy and thanksgiving. We thank you, giver of all gifts and giver of life. We ask that you will watch over *baby's name*. We pray that they might be holy, that they will worship you throughout their life. Allah, may they serve you and come to know you more. Please bless them with opportunity and with wellbeing. Be their God, and may they be your servant. Enable their parents to raise them in the best way, and allow *baby's name* to experience your love and care through the love of their family. We thank you, Allah, for your faithfulness and the great gift of *baby's name*. Ameen.

A Buddhist Prayer

We ring in this day with great cheer. We are so glad that *baby's name* is here; we invite you to smile upon them and bless their life, Oh great Buddha. May they know happiness and peace. May they experience the fullness of joy. May they laugh so wholeheartedly that they know delight in the fullest. May others show them kindness, and may they pay this kindness on to others. May each day hold a gift. May they know peace in the easy moments and in the hard moments. We pray that you bless them and their parents. May life be fuller when blessed with this great and amazing child.

PRAYER FOLLOWING THE DEATH OF A BABY

While joyful prayers can be said over a newborn baby, there are also mournful prayers that can be said when a baby is stillborn or dying soon after birth. The pain experienced when a person is expecting a baby but instead experiences death is something that most people will never understand. It is hard to explain why God would let something like this happen. It is important not to claim to have an answer, or to fake that you understand what they are going through or why God did this. And yet, while you might not be able to provide an answer for why this happened, you can be present to the person and serve as a voice of assurance from God/the Holy. People from various religions believe that God will never abandon a person in these tragic circumstances, and that God is faithful in caring for the unborn baby even in the face of death. It in important while praying in these circumstances to provide assurances of God's presence and mutual sadness, while not glossing over the fact that this is a very painful circumstance. It is rarely comforting for a person to hear that "God needed another angel" or "Everything happens for a reason." You will note that this language is not present in the prayers and should not be used.

A Christian Prayer

Provider God, you are a very present help in times of trouble. You are the one who promises not to leave us, especially on days like today. So, in the midst of this terrible day, where this family is deeply mourning, we pray that you hold them in your comforting care. Jesus, you called children into your arms because you love them so very much. You love *baby's name* so very much and you hold him/her in your tender care. God, I thank you for giving him/her parents that are trying their best to be the best parents they can be even in this hard circumstance. May *baby's name* know that love of her parents and family, and may it surround him/her now. God, we do not know why tragedies like this happen, but we pray that you are welcoming *baby's name* into your arms and caring for him/her, even during death and sorrow. I also pray that you watch out for him/her family that is mourning now. God, give them a comfort that passes our understanding. Walk with them today and in the days, months, and years ahead. May the memory of *baby's name* live on with them. Amen.

A Jewish Prayer

YHWH, giver of shalom, you are the one who promises not to leave us, especially on days like today. So, in the midst of this terrible day, where this family is deeply mourning, we pray that you hold them in your comforting care. God, you call us each a child of God. You love *baby's name*, who your child, and you hold him/her in your tender care. God, I thank you for giving him/her parents that are trying their best to be the best parents they can be even in this hard circumstance. May *baby's name* know that love of her parents and family, and may it surround him/her now. God, we do not know why tragedies like this happen, but we pray that you are welcoming *baby's name* into your arms and caring for him/her, even during death and sorrow. I also pray that you watch out for his/her family that is mourning now. God, give them a comfort that passes our understanding. Walk with them today and in the days, months and years ahead. May the memory of *baby's name* live on with them, as they recite kaddish and as they mourn. Amen.

An Islamic Prayer

Insha'Allah, one who walks with us through the most difficult circumstances and deepest pain. In the midst of this terrible day, where this family is deeply mourning, we pray that you hold them in your comforting care. Prophet, you are the one who can bless and give peace, and we pray for that today. We pray that you bless and keep *baby's name*, and that you also bless his/her parents with peace. They are seeking to be the best parents to this child even in the midst of this very difficult situation. So, we pray that *baby's name* might know their love and be surrounded in this. I also pray that they might know the love that you have for them even in this circumstance. Be with them in the days, months, and years ahead. Amen.

A Buddhist Prayer

Living is suffering and yet we are not without hope in the face of suffering. When the world was formed, when we were formed, when *baby's name* was formed, we and they became part of the same, vast creation. And, so, while we deeply mourn the death of *baby's name,* he/she is still part of creation, and part of the vastness that surrounds us. He/she will live on in the world around us, and bless those who are still here. May those who love her know moments when he/she is surrounding them. O Holy Light, it is a day of suffering and a day in which we need more calm and peace. I ask that this is bestowed on them, and that they might know comfort and grace.

PRAYER TO CALM ANGER

Healthcare workers face a lot of stress, from dealing with patients with difficult personalities, to packed schedules, to conflict with coworkers. While these situations can stir up a lot of emotions, they can often lead to anger. Releasing anger is important for somebody's well being. These prayers aim to help people release what they are holding onto and embrace a more positive attitude. They are prayers that people can pray for themselves. Each religion values the ability to let go of anger, or the temptation to act in anger. These prayers are a reminder of that ideology, as well as a way to step back and tack a deep breath.

A Christian Prayer

God of grace, there are days when I need a little bit of mercy to get through. Today is one of those days. Help ease my anger, and transform it into patience and benevolence. I specifically lift up to you this situation that is causing these hard feelings, and pray that you help me find a solution to *named situation.* Help me see through another's point of view so that I can be more kind and understanding. Let me also offer understanding to myself. Let me release the things that are making me mad, and turn them over to you. Help me see the blessings of today and overcome the challenges. Sometimes feelings seem to control me instead of me being able to control my emotions. Strengthen me and give me exactly what I need in order to act in the grace and love that you show to me each and every day. Amen.

A Jewish Prayer

YHWH-Shalom, giver of peace, show me mercy today so that I might be gracious to others. Anger draws me away from you. Help ease my anger and transform it to patience and benevolence. Help me see through another person's point of view so that I can be more kind and understanding. Bless me to be a blessing. Rid me of any contention, and give me peace and calm. Sometimes feelings seem to control me instead of me being able to control my emotions. Strengthen me and give me what I need to prevail against these difficult emotions. Fill my heart with love so that I can be in relationship with others and with you. Amen.

An Islamic Prayer

Allah, anger is not always bad. It is an emotion, which you have given us, and there are right and good uses for our anger. But that is only righteous anger. But, when our anger controls us and motivates us to think and do bad things, it causes us and others harm. Allah, you are with a One who is patient. So, give me patience and kindness today, as I truly need it. Be with me. Give me understanding. Let me offer benevolence to others and to myself. Give me the strength to do all of these things. Allah, let me have control over my temper so that I do not spoil relationships. Ameen.

A Buddhist Prayer

Anger wounds the world, and so, Higher Power, I seek to release it. May I let go of this destructive feeling. May I embrace a different emotion - one that is more grace-filled and holy. May I offer peace to myself and to others. May I see the bigger picture and live into a more beautiful now. Forgive my anger and may any scars of this anger be erased. With a breath out, may I experience relief from anger. With a breath in, may I experience happiness and joy. May I know freedom from these shackles that are holding me down. Oh, Great Power, lead me to lay my burdens down.

PRAYER TO HELP LET GO OF A DYING LOVED ONE

As a person approaches death, those who stand beside them set about trying to let go. Sometimes a person will hold on to life until those they love most give them permission to die. Again and again, people have waited to hear permissive words from their family or friends before they can leave this world. While it is a difficult task, often letting go is the most loving thing that a person can offer to a person who is dying. And yet, this is a hard task because of our attachment to people. These prayers are ways that people can name their attachment, fear and sadness, and start to give themselves permission to let go. It is commonly believed that it is only God that can give somebody the strength to do a task like this.

A Christian Prayer

Compassionate and omniscient God, you know the number of hairs on our head and the number of days of our lives. And yet, while we know that you hold us tenderly in your loving hands, and guard us in life and in death, it is never easy to say goodbye. This family longs for more days with *person's name*, but they hold that in tension with the fact that they also want *person's name* to have comfort and peace. God, we know that today is not one of peace and comfort for them. So, as they mourn and grieve how short life is, I pray that you help move them through their grief. We thank you for each day and each memory of *person's name's* life, and the way that this world is not the same because they are in it. Help their family say what they need to say, and bless *person's name* with their love and their words. May this time together be a beautiful and gracious goodbye. Amen.

A Jewish Prayer

God of all of our days, you promise to walk with us each day of our lives. You hold us tenderly in your loving care. And yet, on days like today, we cry out to you in sorrow and in pain. We ask for you to hear our cries and answer our tears with words of comfort. It is never easy to say goodbye. This family longs for more memories and days with *person's name*, but they hold that in tension with the fact that they also want *person's name* to have comfort and peace. Today is not a day of comfort or peace, and we know that. So, as they mourn and grieve how short life is, I pray that you help move them through grief. We thank you for each day and each memory of *person's name's* life, and the way that this world is not the same because they are in it. Help their family say what they need to say, and bless *person's name* with their love and their words. Amen.

An Islamic Prayer

Allah, on the judgment day, you will hold us accountable for how we spent our days and used our lives. As *person's name* approaches the end of life, we are more mindful of how we spend this day with them and this day worshipping you. It is never easy to let go and say goodbye, and yet, to spend this day just in sadness would be a waste. We hope to honor *person's name* today, to bless them with assurances of your promises to us, to say the things to them that we need to say, and to bid them goodbye until we meet again. God, I ask that you give their family what they need today, and that this place might be made holy. Make this place holy by allowing this family to let go and to trust in you. May this time together be a beautiful and gracious goodbye. Ameen.

A Buddhist Prayer

Holy Presence, death is not the end. And yet, when faced with death, it is hard to not grieve and to hold onto a person longer than we are intended to. Help this family as they mourn and grieve. May they know the words that they need to say in order to have closure and be able to tell *person's name* that they have permission to move on. May you bless *person's name* today, and may this day be one of peace for them as they reach the end of their life. May you look kindly on their life, and create in them a heart that is at peace. We ask that for each person who stands in this room today.

A PRAYER FOR FORGIVENESS

Throughout life, people do things they wish they had not done, say things they wish they had not said, and think things they wish they had not thought. In many religions, it is thought that these grievances are done not only against people, but also against God. For that reason, they are commonly referred to as sins, and a person must seek forgiveness from God to make it right. This asking is done in prayer.

In various stages of life, we are reminded of the wrongs that we have done; it is at these moments that the pain associated the wrongdoing is fresh and more painful. Often, in a hospital setting, people confront their own sins and wrongdoings with honesty and regret. Being able to say a prayer in which you ask for forgiveness is an important way to care for the whole person – letting go of regret is also an essential part of healing. These prayers aim to help you give words to people's longing for forgiveness.

A Christian Prayer

Almighty God, you are all-powerful, and yet you humbled yourself in order to come into our world in human flesh. As our incarnate Lord, you modeled for us what it looks like to be a disciple here on earth. You showed us what it means to really, truly serve God wholeheartedly, and you joyfully called us to follow your ways. We said that we follow, but when we look back at the various paths we take through life, we realize that we have not always followed your ways. Our thoughts and actions show that we frequently choose to let other things rule over our lives. When that happens, each thing we value above you wedges its way between us and distances us from your presence. Forgive us, Lord, for treading down other paths, rather than following you. Spirit

God, despite all that we have done that is not of your will, you still call us to follow, with the same joyful, grace-filled voice. You advise us to be like children, and to humbly approach your throne. So, almighty God, we come to you with bowed heart and humbled spirit, asking for your forgiveness. We are your children, and you are our father. Restore out hope in you. Reclaim the center of our lives. Direct our feet down your paths. Claim us in our entirety. Specifically, we pause in silence as we each confess the things that we have done, silently to you. Forgive our sins. Amen.

A Jewish Prayer

Merciful God, we bow before you, offering up our wrongdoings and asking that you cleanse us from all unrighteousness. You have shown us what is good and right, and we had instead chosen to do what is wrong and unjust. Our thoughts and actions show that we frequently put other idols above you. So, gracious God, we ask that you look upon us with grace and make us new. Reclaim the center of our lives. Direct our feet down the right paths. Specifically, we pause in just this moment of silence to confess to you the sins and grievances that are on our heart. God, take these away for us and restore our souls. Amen.

An Islamic Prayer

Allah, our lord, we have wronged you, our fellow humans, our world, and our selves. We have done things we should never have done, thought things we should never have thought, and said things we should have never said. *Person's name* is harboring guilt for specific wrongs done in their lives, and hoping that you will be gracious and forgive. You, Allah, are full of mercy and when we come to you, you will not turn us away. So, I pray that you take away the weight that is lying on *person's name*, and instead fill it with your calm and peace. Ameen.

A Buddhist Prayer

I have done harm to myself, to others, to the world, and to the Holy. I have not lived in the way that I wish I had lived. Allow me to forgive myself and be gracious with myself. May I also choose to live differently and embrace a way of loving kindness. May I seek to right the wrongs that I have done. May I live more fully, and more respectfully – honoring myself and others. May any weight or guilt be removed from my shoulder so that I might live in freedom. May it be so.

A PRAYER FOR EASING PAIN

As patients battle cancer, heal from trauma, or face other ailments, pain management is a critical part of their care. Often pain can reach a point that it is too much to bear and a person can lose hope. It is in these moments that the Holy can be asked to ease a person's pain. There are many cases of prayer, not medication, being what eases a person's pain. Pain can be spiritual and psychological, just as much as it can be physical. Moreover, if the pain has a physical root, acknowledging the pain in a spiritual practice can help a person overcome it. Frequently people will say that it is only God that heals, and so recognizing this in patient care is essential. It is also a way to compassionately recognize the suffering that people are facing. As you pray, you are proclaiming that you see the person in their pain and that they are not alone.

A Christian Prayer

Great Physician, when you were here on earth, people would come from near and far to experience relief from their symptoms and be miraculously healed. Miracles are not a thing of the past, and you do not leave us alone in our pain. So, today we ask that you relieve *person's name* of their pain. Give them rest and comfort. Allow the medicines to work, and for them to start feeling better immediately. Also, please take away any emotional or spiritual burdens that are contributing to their pain. Give them freedom of spirit as you free them from the pains that are holding them down. Be the miracle worker that we believe you to be, and come quickly, Lord Jesus. Amen.

A Jewish Prayer

YHWH, you are the only one who can heal us. So, we pray for healing for *person's name.* Your breath gave life to the first humans, and it is your breath that can restore *person's name* now. May you take away any pain they are experiencing and give them the deep sighs of relief that accompany comfort. Give them rest and relief. Allow the medicines to work so that they might feel better immediately. Please take away any emotional or spiritual burdens that are contributing to their pain. Give them freedom of spirit as you free them from the pains that are burdening them. Just as you supplied manna for hungry people in the desert, provide for *person's name's* needs today. Amen.

An Islamic Prayer

Ar-Ra'uf, kind God, you give us gifts when we most need them. Today, *person's name* needs relief from the pain. Give them comfort and relief. Allow the medicine to work so that they might feel better as soon as possible. May they have the rest that they need to heal, and the comfort that they need to get that rest. Take away their symptoms that are causing distress and instead give them peace. Be the comforting God that we know you to be and hold them tenderly in your compassionate care. Take away any ailment, and let them achieve full recovery soon. Amen.

A Buddhist Prayer

This world holds so much beauty, but also so much suffering. Great Buddha, you taught us to pursue comfort by meditating and changing the way we experience the suffering of the world. May you guide *person's name* today as they attempt to find comfort in the midst of their pain. As they focus on the parts of their body where they need relief, send light and love to provide them comfort and care. May he/she have rest and peace. Fill them from the inside out and restore their soul and body. May light shine from their core and greet the world with hope.

A PRAYER FOR CHANGES IN ONE'S LIFE

There are many ways that a person's life can change in a hospital setting. Some of the biggest and most tragic changes to experience are becoming paraplegic, dealing with brain damage and altered mental status, and/or amputations. However, while these are drastic changes, any change can be drastic for a person. Whenever we lose the ability to do something that we once could do, we become a different person than we were. Changes can lead to fear, anxiety, and a changed perspective on who we are. A person's identity is a central component to their practice of religion, so is it important to recognize these challenges and changes of their own self in their religious practices. This can give validity to their feelings, and help them express their grief. God meets people in this grief.

A Christian Prayer

Creator God, you made us each uniquely with our gifts, abilities, and personality. You have made *person's name* uniquely and gave them their skills. They have grown into their own identity throughout their life, and became accustomed to the person that they were. That is why it is hard to face these changes that have come recently. It is a huge change. *Person's name* is facing what it means to be a changed person, and to lose the *named change*. As they figure out with who they are now, I pray that you help them restore any abilities that they are able to regain. Make them a new creation. And, whatever cannot be healed or changed, I pray that you use it for the best. May you strengthen *patient's name*, and give them patience with themselves as they seek to confront the stresses and strains that life has held. May they grow further into who they are now and appreciate who they still uniquely are now. Also, hear their grief and provide comfort. Amen.

A Jewish Prayer

Creator God, you made us each uniquely with our gifts, abilities, and personality. You have made *person's name* uniquely and gave them their abilities. They have grown into their own identity throughout their life, and became accustomed to the person that they were. That is why it is hard to face these changes that have come recently. It is a huge change. *Person's name* is facing what it means to be a changed person, and to lose the *named change*. As they figure out with who they are now, I pray that you help them restore any abilities that they are able to regain. And, whatever cannot be healed or changed, I pray that you use it for the best. May you strengthen *patient's name*, and give them patience with themselves as they seek to confront the stresses and strains that life has held. May they grow further into who they are now and appreciate who they still uniquely are. Also, hear their grief and provide comfort. Amen.

An Islamic Prayer

Al-Khaliq, Creator, you made us each uniquely with our gifts, abilities, and personality. You have made *person's name* uniquely and gave them their abilities. They have grown into their own identity throughout their life, and became accustomed to the person that they were. That is why it is hard to face these changes that have come recently. It is a huge change. *Person's name* is facing what it means to be a changed person, and to lose the *named change*. As they figure out with who they are now, I pray that you help them restore any abilities that they are able to regain. We know dua and worship can change your heart and pray that your heart and this person's destiny is changed. And, whatever cannot be healed or changed, I pray that you use it for the best. May you strengthen *patient's name*, and give them patience with themselves as they seek to confront the stresses and strains that life has held. May they grow further into who they are now and appreciate who they still uniquely are now. Also, hear their grief and provide comfort. Amen.

A Buddhist Prayer

We have plans and expectations of what we want our life to be. It is hard when what we expect and what we appreciate is taken away. It is hard to let go. And yet, Buddha has taught us that letting go can lead to greater peace. Today we hope to let go, and to find peace. And yet, that is not an easy endeavor. So, as *patient's name* is having such trouble facing these challenges, may they know a peace and calm in the midst of the storm. As a slow breath calms the spirit, may their practice of prayer calm them and give them the strength to face the challenges of today. May they embrace who they are now, who they were, and who they will be.

A PRAYER OF THANKSGIVING

Most of these prayers are about the harder moments in life, but prayers are not just for difficult times. Prayer is also a way to praise God for the good things that happen in life. While pain and sickness are within hospital walls, healing and a new chance on life also happen. These are equally important to recognize in prayer. If we just go to God in prayer to ask for things, God becomes a "vending machine God." A vending machine God dispenses answers to prayer requests in the same way that a vending machine will give you what you want when you press the right button. Instead, for most religions, God is one in which we are relationship, not just a God to be approached when we need something.

A Christian Prayer

Great and wonderful God, we come to you with thanksgiving today! Thank you so much for healing *patient's name*, and for restoring their health. While it has been a long journey, you brought them through it. We know that you are the source of each good gift, and do not forget that today. We hope that this is a just the beginning of many good days of health. In each of these days, we praise you. We know that you are good and that you are working things out for good for all. We thank you for seeing those glimpse of light and love today. Amen.

A Jewish Prayer

HaShem, blessed God, we thank you for your blessings and for your kindness. We especially thank you for healing *patient's name*, and for getting them through this hard time. It is you who brought them through, just as you have brought all people through all things throughout all of history. You are the source of each good gift, and we remember that this morning. We hope that this is the beginning of many more days of good health. May these words of praise rise to you today. As the sun rises on a new day, may our renewed and appreciative understanding of you shed light on our world and our soul. Amen.

An Islamic Prayer

Al-Muhyi, giver of life, Al-Mu'id, restorer of life, it is you who has restored *patient's name's* health. Allah, you are the one who has given this gift and so we return thanks to you. We hope that this is the beginning of many brighter days ahead. May they use their health to do good in the world. May they be blessed today and in turn bless others. We thank you for all of creation and for what you are creating in our lives. May each good thing rise to you as a sweet sacrifice and aroma for praise. Ameen.

A Buddhist Prayer

Buddha and Bodhisattvas, this life contains such good things. We are thankful for these things, and especially for *patient's name's* healing. We take a moment to recognize this blessing. We also hope that it is not just in these good moments that we are grateful and at peace. We hope that in the ups and downs of life that we hold onto the appreciation and calm that the Buddha carried through life. Oh Holy Light, we hold onto this moment and recognize the beauty that life holds. May we rest in this blessing and greet this gift, just as we greet each thing this world has to offer.

A PRAYER WHEN LEAVING THE HOSPITAL

As people leave the hospital, they set out on a new journey. Sometimes this journey is greeted with great joy and thanksgiving. This is often the case when the person is healed and going home to a clean slate. In contrast and sometimes at the same time, sometimes going home is marked by fear or discomfort. When the patient is leaving to go to assisted living, rehab, or does not know next steps for their healthcare- leaving can look different. Blessing the person through prayer as they step into the next steps is something that religious practices can offer to each of these cases.

A Christian Prayer

God of new beginnings, this day marks the start of a new step and a new stage on this path. We thank you for bringing them this far and ask that you walk with them in this next step. We are thankful for the healing they have experienced to be able to leave the hospital, and pray for continued healing for them. As they step out of this hospital, go ahead of them, making a way. Walk beside them, giving them assurance. Walk behind them, giving them peace around where they have been. God, be the one who surrounds them and blesses them. I pray that this next step goes smoothly, and that you calm any fear that they have. Give them things to look forward to. Amen.

A Jewish Prayer

Holy and Righteous God, God of new beginnings, this day marks the start of a new step and a new stage on this path. We thank you for bringing them this far and ask that you walk with them in this next step. We are thankful for the healing they have experienced to be able to leave. You are the one who guided people in the desert, and along many rocky and windy roads. You are also the one who walks with people as they rejoice. So, I pray that you are with *person's name* each step of the way. As they step out of this hospital, go ahead of them, making a way. Walk beside them, giving them assurance. Walk behind them, giving them peace around where they have been. God, be the one who surrounds them and blesses them. I pray that this next step goes smoothly, and that you calm any fear that they have. Give them things to look forward to. Amen.

An Islamic Prayer

Al-Wakil, God in whom we trust, we put our faith in you as we start the first steps of this next journey. This day holds new beginnings, and with that we put our trust in you. So, I pray that you are with *person's* name each step of the way. As they step out of this hospital, go ahead of them, making a way. Walk beside them, giving them assurance. Walk behind them, giving them peace around where they have been. God, be the one who surrounds them and blesses them. I pray that this next step goes smoothly, and that you calm any fear that they have. Give them things to look forward to. And each step of the way may they come to know you more. Amen.

A Buddhist Prayer

Today is a day of new beginnings. With hope, we greet it. May *patient's name*'s steps be blessed. May they walk with ease throughout the world. May each step of their journey hold insight and understanding as they grow more and more into who they are and will be. May blessings shower them and bless them. With a small moment of silence, we greet a new start. We turn over any anxiety; we let go of expectations. We offer ourselves to the universe and to the holy light.

Dear Reader,

If you enjoyed this book or found it useful, I would be very grateful if you would post a short review on Amazon. Your support really does make a difference and I read all the reviews personally so I can get your feedback and make this book even better.

If you are a member of kindleunlimited, I would be most grateful if you would scroll to the back of the book so I will be paid for your borrowed book.

Thanks again for your support.

America Selby

Please leave a review
Go to amazon.com and type in
America Selby to find my books.

Made in the USA
Middletown, DE
22 October 2023

41265886R00029